ABOUT THE AUTHOR

Maria Marshall was born in Shepherds Bush, London, in 1935, to Alice and Edward Dalton, from Co. Westmeath; he died in 1940 from TB. Her sister Veronica was born in June that year. Alice's siblings Angela and Joseph both married and were close and supportive during the difficult war years.

Maria married Peter Marshall in 1956 and they had three daughters – Tessa, Noreen and Mairead. She has eight grandchildren and two great-grandchildren. After her retirement from teaching Business Studies in London, Maria and Peter moved to Ireland in 1999 to be close to two daughters and their families. Following an inspiring six-week writing course by writer Grace Wells in 2009, Maria was one of the founder members of the Loughboy Writers Group in Kilkenny.

Maria self-published *A Child's War* in 2016 – her memories of living in London throughout World War II.

Maria Marshall

MEANDERING IDEAS

AUSTIN MACAULEY PUBLISHERS™
LONDON • CAMBRIDGE • NEW YORK • SHARJAH

A CIP catalogue record for this title is available from the British Library.

ISBN 9781398436213 (Paperback)
ISBN 9781398436220 (ePub e-book)

www.austinmacauley.com

First Published 2021
Austin Macauley Publishers Ltd
1 Canada Square
Canary Wharf
London
E14 5AA

DEDICATION

Dedicated to my beloved husband Peter who encouraged me in every way during our 64 years together.

POEMS

WHAT IS A POEM?

Attempt to capture the sublime,
stretch across the gulf of time
a tapestry of threaded thoughts
arising from the depths unbidden
to reach the ears of the unknown.
Thirst for immortality,
fragments from a feeling heart
reveal what is concealed, apart.
Surge of clues to share deep joy
else express life's hidden woes,
impressions of a deep desire
to spread out into endless space
lacy fragments of forgotten dreams;
expressions of a spirit's need
to leave an echo of self behind.

A – ART

BETRAYAL

(based on "The Taking of Christ" by Caravaggio.
See RTE Documentary "Masterpiece – The Taking of Christ")

Stony earth like the core of man,
no friendly frieze of shining stars,
moon ashamed to show its face,
garden draped in darkness
designed to shroud foul deeds,
resentful needs to innocence destroy.

Bright-faced artist shines a light,
rays divine rest on one face,
eyes shut in sorrowful unbelief,
hands folded in the way of grief,
first of many cuts to come,
His final journey has begun.

One friend remains, outstretched hand,
spirit shrinking, terror stricken,
desperate to silently slip away,
courage gone, like all the other
friends – scattered like sheep astray.

One-time friend, hardened heart
with grasping greed o'ertaken,
loyalty forsaken, a glassy eye
reflecting the lure of shiny silver;
a kiss – of all the signs to use,
chilling abuse from so-called friend.

Silence shattered by clinking swords,
sinister sheen of gleaming armour.
Followers dreaming of a king
to free them from the physical foe,
how could they know, a spiritual king
would later send them understanding
and free their fettered minds forever.

SHAKESPEARE – getting to know him

["Let me not to the marriage of true minds admit impediment.
Love is not love which alters when it alteration finds"]

Let me not shirk the task of tackling Shakespeare –
the one who understanding of the human psyche doth show.
Whether one soul, or cultured combination
he peered into the very heart of each
and showered forth a spate of splendid words,
uncovered the face behind the mask, a task
to kindle interest, stir sleeping emotions,
unlock our understanding and compassion;
gifted gatherer of tales conveying truths.
Remember the relentless march of time and tide,
depart from spheres of fear and hesitation,
delve deep and sure into his treasure chest –
the best, and worst, of human kind is there
to teach us much – if only we can dare.

SHELTER

I turn it over in my mind, ponder what it means,
seems so soft and smooth within my moving mouth,
unborn babe image within the womb emerges unbidden,
hidden within the watery bed which cushions her from harm,
where she is gently rocked and soothed by the beat of a loving heart.

A tender painting of a little child comes gently from the past
bent over a little brook to pick a solitary flower,
unaware of any snare a sudden slip could cause her,
but, faintly shimmering in the summer air, an angel fair
stands with outstretched wings sheltering his small charge.

As for myself I know the refuge of my inner world
where I can shelter, small and curled, until the storm abates
and life creates another worthwhile challenge for the day.

B – TIME & SPACE

TIME

A structure stretching into years,
flatly trapped upon the calendar face,
yet exists a flowing circle of seasons
which coil and turn like tornadoes spinning,
teaching mankind a host of reasons

to watch and till, sow, reap and plan,
use his precious time as best he can.
Yet deep within us is a graceful presence
that recognises no limits, knows no bounds –
an un-chained awe-inspiring essence.

Like shore-hugging sand time shifts and moves
and proves its constant, pressurising presence
in waves which ebb and flow with casual ease;
it flows and comes and goes, and disappears,
washed clear away by the waters of life.

Each person whether King or fool
is governed by its unremitting rule;
we often quote that "Love's not time's fool"
and yet for many it proves to be the case –
ground down or lost in life's careering race.

Father figure scything lives,
reaper stepping in with sickle sharp;
we have been warned, we know not time nor hour,
just told when our time is up by the boatman in charge
"Time, please" – like some punctilious barman.

OUT THERE BEYOND

Men always sought to scan the velvet spread of sky
and nearer bring the sequins ever-sparkling there,
wove stories of the souls who twinkled still,
revelled in the ordered way they moved around,
found the secret pictures hidden there.

Traced in delight the Gemini twins, the Plough, the Crab.
Knew our bright star the Sun was our essential
source of light and life to every living thing.
They doubted not the wonder of her silver sister Moon
who nightly bathes in her reflected glory.

Men reverenced that special Star which brought the Kings;
it stopped and humbly hovered over a stable of light;
that Silent Night the world was changed for evermore.
They chorused praise and raised voices up to heaven.

When rocket ships and satellites journeyed into space
THEY turned us to face a different view of Earth;
since then our gaze ever outward further probing.
Now nations race, they have a thirst to be the first
Columbus setting forth to claim a Newer World.

Voyager started the longest journey ever taken
two whole years and half-a-billion miles;
approached the giant Jupiter, mighty King of the Gods,
sent a magical stream of startling pictures;
then, a planet whose massive mouth could swallow all the rest –
baleful Red Globe of endless raging storm,
born from violent events 4-billion years ago.

Continued

As far away again was found giant Saturn,
gas balloon surrounded by its 18 moons,
encircled by a thick and multi-layered ring –
truly beautiful bangle of hurtling fragments and dust,
whirling ring of rocks, a super spinning wheel.
Only artists' work can flood our souls with joy;
the scientific facts may feed our rational minds
but marvellous as these are, the inner spirit smiles –
complex explanations merely uncover deeper mystery –
our human history shown to be so very brief –
a mini-verse in the multi-volume story of creation.

The mind-boggling miracle of our stupendous solar system,
gigantic galaxy containing countless clustering stars
turns out to be but one of many millions existing
in that vast, uncharted, stretch of waterless sea.

We thought we knew a little of His mighty creative ways.
The mockers jeer "He made the Earth in seven days!"
Remember and echo Gibran whose mystic words insisted
"If just *one* star, *one* flower alone had been created"
what wondrous proof of our Creator's deft design.

A single star, like us, is born only to die;
after aeons of brilliance, explodes like a giant balloon,
sending waves of shock shooting and spreading around;
furious inferno burning 10-million years,
causing clouds of dust to mould into scores of worlds;
only some survived the impact of violent space.
Also triggered was the harsh and hellish birth of our Sun
till she transformed to the "smile of light" which gifted Earth.

Continued

Over endless lengths of time planets gradually formed –
giant Jupiter and paternal Saturn swelled in size,
greedily sucking icy debris from the abyss.
When we gaze transfixed at these unbelievable images
we stare-and-stare, dumb-founded, and when we've had our fill
we know the God who made our Earth is mightier still.
When we "in awesome wonder consider all the works
His mighty hands have made – the stars, the rolling thunder
His wondrous works throughout the Universe displayed",
then from the heart we sing "My God how great thou art!"

THE TRAVELLER (the Ice Man)

(Sept. 1991 Similaun Glacier, Italian border, an ancient well-preserved body found, and named Otzi.)

He lay alone unseeing and unsung,
he lay inert for five thousand years,
folded in a hollow, foetus-like, although
high upon the steep Alpine slopes,
reverently enshrined in a slim shroud of snow.
No written words about him have been found
and yet he left a thousand clues to build
a picture of his time and life, his strife
in the face of serious wound and fierce weather
which, together, overcame his strength and skill,
his will to carry on his lonesome trip.

He came from a time of kinder climate;
we've learnt the range of trees that grew back then –
hazel, ash, birch and larch, yew, lime;
sloeberry has shown the time of year was autumn,
seeds show signs of laburnum and dogswood
and an ancient type of wheat from an early farm.
His bow was yew with two arrows primed,
twelve more half-made in leather quiver,
small grass bag, mushrooms for tinder,
backpack of hazel and a fire striker,
axe and leather pouch with flint scraper,
flint knife with handle of ashwood.

Continued

Only in limited areas can that flint be found
and even the leather holds secrets of its own –
its type and how it has been treated and tanned.
He had walked and climbed the mountain paths alone,
well prepared for his hazardous journey home,
carrying his brown container of birch bark.
Further armed with a fine copper sword
and a rope, he wore a tunic of patched leather,
his grass cape around his shoulders slung,
boots of leather stuffed with grass for warmth.
He stood five feet two, a man in his twenties.

We can see him striding along the winding way
but – weak from his arrow wound and caught off guard
by sudden swirling storm, he laid him down
where he found a concave hollow in the ground
and curled up small between two rocky ridges.
By all the known rules of glacier flow
he should have gradually drifted far below
but Fate decreed his chosen hiding place
would keep him dry and free from interference.

Sun and wind dried, and covered with snow,
then Sahara storm blew a blanket of dust;
no birds or foxes enjoyed his freezing flesh
or stripped and gnawed his solitary bones.
Questions about this man are never ending;
we wonder from where the lonely traveller came
and what was his intended destination.
Maybe he was a lakeman from the north,
maybe he had travelled south to Italian hills
rarely rich in a precious type of flint,
likely to be a familiar route for him,
and was wending his difficult way homeward.

Continued

Lake Constanz was inhabited 6k years ago,
houses on piles, walls of wattle and daub.
Dwellers of that time had roofs of bark.
The Ice Man could be their descendant.
His Ice Maiden sister had been found
in the bleak cold of South Siberian Mountains –
a nomadic warrior, she, who hunted from horseback,
knowing the power of bow and arrow like him
but She was two thousand years his junior.

On other pages of history on his Continent
bog bodies were brothers half his age
but left no guts or brains for us to study –
and Greenland Eskimos though well-preserved
were very young – a mere 500 years.
The scientific search delves evermore deep
our curiosity unlikely to be curbed;
the Ice Man's sleep continues to be disturbed
though we would like to see him Rest in Peace.

Lake Constanz –
where Germany,
Austria and
Switzerland meet

THE MOON

Graceful crescent arc appears
gazing on our shadowy world,
mantled by her Milky Way gown
she carries aloft a star-studded crown.
Throne supported by the starry throng
crystal sparks once lost souls.
Luminous figure gradually growing,
mother waiting for fulfilment.
Rhythms of life ebb and flow
as she steadily sweeps across the skies,
beams on her subjects spread below
who gaze on her with worshipping eyes
while drawing out powers of creation –
but some minds stumble over the abyss.
Like us, she has a darker side
when all that beauty's dimmed and grey;
all that's bright seems to have died,
rays of truth secreted away;
that curtain of grey can mask her from view.
With bated breath the watchers wait
till she re-appears, a glowing bride,
visage unwrinkled, radiant, young;
a soothing face to gaze upon
unlike her sizzling sister Sun.
When her reign of glory is over,
finally deflated, she gently gives view
to a newborn babe crescent in shape
starting the cycle of life anew.

NEW YEAR

New-born year struggles through
birth canal of hectic Christmas celebration,
arrives unblemished, free of fear or terror,
un-besmirched by past mistakes or error,
unaware of all our failed resolves.
Arms outstretched, spontaneous eagerness
sparking hope to help us strive anew.
We marvel at serene, unmarked brow,
slowly shed the sorrows of the
past, newly-completed cycle of the seasons,
approach with faith a clean slate on which
to chalk our newly risen hopes & dreams.

C – SUFFERING & LOSS

ALONE

He had so much to live for, a wife who cared for him,
children close to him, yet suffered isolation.
He left alone.

A black cloud above, inner desolation
no pills could dispel, painful inner hell.
He left alone.

He knew that he was loved but suffered dark depression,
a deep well of night, intolerable burden.
He left alone.

Constantly weighed down, not feeling up to the task,
happy feelings gone, not able to go on.
He left alone.

He'd taught his children much but still felt out of touch
to such a painful extent, he left without warning.
He left alone.

We visited the river, shivered with chill feelings,
floated be-candled wreath, imagined him beneath.
He left alone.

We gathered for the mourning. His daughter wrote a poem –
a husband who was loving, a father who was caring –
but he left alone.

We dream of a new dawning, a bright cloudless morning,
no heavy load to carry, no piercing doubts to parry,
no longer left alone.

HOMELESS

Out and down in Dublin town,
young and old in cramping cold,
somebody's father, mother, or son.
Windswept street, little to eat,
violent gangs, hunger pangs;
hang a notice, nil by mouth.

No fixed abode, no money for rent,
cardboard boxes make a tattered tent,
derelict doorways, unsafe buildings,
any hole, in deep despair.
Some like to accuse of slyly faking
or say "their plight is of their making".

Nothing to do, nowhere to go,
pace of life painful and slow,
roam in the park, sleep on benches,
summer sun burns, winter rain drenches,
holey socks, leaking shoes,
shiver and shake, asleep or awake.
Sleeping bag, be-spattered and torn,

onion layers attempt to keep warm.
Need a drink to warm the bones
sharing seems a way of caring;
need something to stop one sink
into a bone-cold eternal sleep.

Knuckles rapped, energy zapped;
run of soup helps re-coup,
short-lived feel of stomach warmth,
a fraction of our long-lost strength.
Under-rate, not feeling great,
under-valued, under par,
under-fed, that's how we are.

Continued

Drifting dream of a sheltered place,
secure from harm, away from the past.
The Issues Big, who cares a fig?
Can only hope some action's taken
so folk like us are not forsaken –
soon – before we give up hope.

THE GRAVESIDE

*(Nana's grave – one year on – 6/3/99; dedicated to Mark.
"Grant us all Lord your protection the day long of this short life until the shadows
lengthen and our work is done. Grant us all a safe lodging in our heavenly home at last.
Amen" Newman)*

Head bent, thoughts intent, busy levelling the uneven ground;
head bent, re-living times spent; dis-lodging lumps of brick found.
Hands move, sift soil, spreading it with loving care,
like incense on the altar steps, gently but firmly pressing it down.

Head bowed, remembering well the spirit un-cowed in the mortal shell;
kneeling there, on the soil bare, accepting the loved one is free from care,
offering a heart-felt voiceless prayer that rises into the rain-laden air,
grieving still, yet spirit at peace, though knowing the loss will never cease.

Body leaning, spirit keening: dig a hole, plant a flower,
cover its roots, heel it in, so inner healing can begin;
feeling a gamut of emotions but dealing with them face-to-face
knowing grief is no dis-grace.

Knees bent on the velvet moss, multi memories of times past,
action soothing the sense of loss. Experience of life teaches one more –
"counting blessings" makes good sense, of all the gains un-realised,
not recognised in the usual score – a Special Angel for ever-more.

THE CEMETERY

(Bolingbroke Grove, Battersea)

Mouldy monuments of stone stand silent guard
over docile dormitories in this grave yard;
wards of well-kept beds with silent inmates,
bordered with sunken surrounds of eroded stone –

pitted and pocked by decades of rain and storm,
from countless winds and sleet well-worn down,
like the burdened lives of those who now lie sleeping
finished with this finite world of joy or weeping.

Who knows what individual crosses they bore,
pierced by sharply cruel words and deeds,
mis-used, abused, rejected – just like Him
but, unlike Him, self-stained with human sin.

Remains chained in a lonely though lovely abode,
THEY are free from the cracked mirror of early dreams;
their surging spirits escaped on wings unbroken
to join the joyous throng whose song's unspoken.

Mortal shells cocooned for evermore
books opened at an ever-lasting page,
heart-rending words of love and loss,
heart-melting phrases of remembrance.

A peaceful place for a walk, or muted talk,
benches to sit and ponder, deep in thought,
in staff-less wards with echoes from the past,
no time for tears, no further need for fears
- in this quiet comer they Rest in Peace at last.

INCARCERATION

(Wandsworth Prison – dedicated to Babs; Biggs* famous escapee)

Gazing up at grey, gigantic walls –
depressing symbol of incarceration.
A hidden nation of our country's "losers" –
the thoughtless thief, the addict, the dis-content,
the sick in soul or mind left untreated,
persecuted with unheard muted voices
mixed with those inclined to angry choices.
A tall over-powering wall within a wall
designed to ensure nobody follows Biggs*
onto a "removal" van so aptly named.

Enormous doors of studded structure,
set in a modern version of city walls,
enclose endless cells squat and squalid.
Inner walls topped with cage-like mesh
invisibly sift the spirits of those within.
High-towered mill grinds grim power.
But spider centre, with web-like paths outstretched,
is shiny bright for VIPs to see;
sections with cells well-hidden from their view,
nose-wrinkling odours kept at bay.

Families and friends fill the Visitors' Centre –
a bright oasis outside that dismal estate.
Some show a cheerful accustomed face,
others ground down just by the thought
of being in that dark accursed place.
Walk and wait, then walk with burdened heart
longing for the dreaded visit to start.
The slow procession crawls its snail-like way
through weary wait and check, and wait again
and then through search and screen and sniffing hound,
avoiding the searching eyes of those around.

Continued

Heavy hearts pound, steps resound
on sordid step-worn flags of gloomy grey,
surroundings which hardly see the light of day.
As for all the inmates that dwell therein
we tend to think of them as different from us
but truth to tell we could be just the same
but for quirks of fate or grace of God.

Grey walls, ever inward pressing,
encroach on one's very inner being,
atmosphere ever spirit-suppressing,
poaches upon freedom's precious years,
entombs soul, nurtures inmost fears.
Wardens too, walled in by petty rules,
some minds, soured by the grinding regime,
use and abuse their Little Hitler power,
guarding grimly, overseeing fools
who've passed their personal power to the winds.

Barred cupboard, a hermit's cell unchosen
but unlike him it must be shared with others.
Common courtesy here no longer expected,
a trio stripped of basic privacy
forget how it feels to be respected.
The closest of close friends would find it hard –
but horror of horrors with strangers to be barred;
ever inspected insects under glass.

23 hours of locked-up frustration,
what chance is there of joy or useful creation;
full of doubt when outcomes are unknown;
cell pacing, mind spacing out,
completely cut-off from that world outside –
contained in dreams. |It seems no aim in view;
pale images of home slowly dim,
insidious seeds slowly but surely sown
- and then but an hour to stretch lethargic limbs.

Continued

One cheerless day followed by another,
aimless days to drag one spiralling down.
Workless hours of boredom deep and dense.
Hard to feel that one should even bother,
yet courageous spirits try to stay uncowed.
What sense in squeezing spirits down so low
they cannot dwell on any mortal thing.
Often when cages open, birds cannot fly
on weakened, clipped, unused wings –
they've lost the skill to rise towards the sky.

Why has a person landed in this place?
Pulse of fate, or pre-destined date
or could some choices of path or friend
have helped to lead to this dead end?
The needy child still lurks within,
completely enclosed by essential defences,
still un-awakened to his own potential.
Macho mask makes life seem more bearable
cannot take the risk of tearing it off
and baring one's being to outer view.

If only one could learn self-love, to heal
and soothe the scarring wounds of long ago
and hope and pray for mind to be content
to find one's joy in life in simple things
and finally unbind one's wings – to fly
and soar above the unsafe world of past.

UNWANTED

Stoop or kneel, struggle to uproot
unwanted weeds and past thoughts.
Sturdy green heads determined to root
and reach sunward.
Unwanted, inconvenient, struggle alone,
risking all, right to life ignored;
precarious existence, tramping a continent,
dignity un-respected, unrecognised or cared for.
Parched soil, neglected, burnt;
nutrients washed away or blown to smithereens.
But life-forms thrust through
obstacles of war and want;
poppy masses magically re-appear.
Pulse of life throbs slow but strong
to gain at least a foothold.

D – BELIEF

NOW

Now is the moment we have within our hand,
yester-day has gone for ever-more,
no need for dwelling on the painful past,
hoarding hurtful memories in our inner store.
Now is the time to take a positive stand,
forget that wound, forgive that wrong at last,
decide destructive anger to relinquish
and turn it into energetic action,
not let the precious flame of love extinguish.

Now is the moment still within our power,
this precious point in time for us to use,
not glancing back but dwelling on this hour.
Regrets or self-reproach no fruit can bear
but at our spiritual self destructively tear.
No point in feeling guilt, from the past we learn,
dig deep, draw out the deeply rooted kernel,
examine and enter in a spiritual journal,
accept, and find the peace for which we yearn.

Now is the moment within our grasp we hold,
to fritter away, or leave unused, unspent;
the talent buried deep, a treasure untold.
We need to unfold, or sometimes take a tumble
to disallow our earlier dreams to crumble.
Now is the only moment we truly own;
prize it and use it in the wisest way;
positive images will help us mould and hone
our negative pattern of thought to positive sway.

Continued

Accept that life difficult is meant to be;
when we open our eyes to that, then we are free.
Now is the time to write that reluctant line,
that oft-intended note to state our love.
Our dealings should reveal the Dove above;
from our resentment we need to seek release,
allow our Maker to sooth our aching wounds,
smooth away our sorrows, calm our fears,
wipe our tears, re-kindle the joy we need
whatever our sex or station, race or creed.

LET MORNING COME

When sadness penetrates our inner source
and life becomes bereft of meaning
let morning come.

When loss stalks our sombre steps
and disappointment delves into our depths
let morning come.

When death's icy fingers
curl around someone we love
let morning come.

When depression lays a heavy load
darkens and flattens our faltering spirits
let morning come.

When faith succumbs to hapless despair
hard to believe that God is there
let morning come.

When every single step is hard to take
but must be forced for others' sake
let morning come.

When deep-dark dreaded night surrounds us
and deafening silence seeps into our soul
let morning come.

But
when seeds of hope start spurting into life
and Faith awakens in our deeper being
Then morning comes.

SEARCHING

Scanning the starry sky
can we unshroud a Creator's presence,
solve the mystery of ourselves,
or searching within, can we skim away
layers of accumulated guilt, the silt spread unseen
by eons of dogmatic rule.
The arduous school of life decrees deep-set honesty.

Searching through the labyrinthine years –
the fears passed on, rigid rules,
narrow views, cut-and-dried conclusions;
fusions of disturbing mystery woven
throughout embroidered scraps of history.

If new enlightening scrolls appear
or change of author found, what should we fear?
Perhaps the swell of human pride, the Pharisee within
that writes the script to fit the "politicians" role,
forgetting soul.

Searching our souls, though often sore,
they do not heed the fettering bonds
that bind our pondering minds
but once uncovered, bask in the sheer mystery
of being here at all.

SPIRITUAL ARMOUR

Eph. 6. v.10-18

Precious golden girdle of truth
defence against all ruth-less-ness
from without or from within.

Right thinking to protect the breast
and the human heart within
and the soul so prone to sin.

Delicate feet by the spirit-smith shod
strengthened by the peace of God
guided along their rightful path.

Burnished shield of faith sun-bright
too brilliant for demons to behold
quenching the fiery darts so bold.

Winged helmet to hoist us high
save us from the chasm below
and point us t'wards the heavenly sky.

Flashing sword reflecting light
shining through the darkest night
beacon of the Word of God.

Accept the armour of the Lord
stand strong and rooted to the earth
and ever watchful to the end.

AUTUMN OF LIFE

The autumn of life can be sad or fulfilling,
life's journey has tossed us this way and that,
never knowing quite what to expect,
who we will meet, where we will rest.
If open-minded and always willing
to constantly learn from every contact
and how to adjust how we act, then
we're one with all God-made creation –
not always in tune with man's innovation;
just face our tests of crises and clashes,
through challenges rife with joy or strife,
increasingly aware of His/Her presence
whether in wakening or in our dreaming;
accepting our need for deep redeeming.
Dust to dust, ashes to ashes, East to West,
pole to pole, as part of the cosmos,
our honoured role – to show respect for every soul.

E – KILKENNY

RIVER NORE and HER SISTERS

She springs forth from far-off Clonakenny,
smoothly saunters a slim and slender way,
nourished by sleepy sister streams, swelling as she goes,
pushing on keenly, as if her way she somehow knows.
She ambles a jumbled alphabetic way through many places –
Borris and Ballyragget to Castletown and Durrow.

After forcibly channelled to narrow spaces, on she races
past farm and field, golden corn and rich-brown furrow.
Then lovingly loops into Inistioge, historic gem,
while swans gracefully glide, ducks head-dip and waddle;
dainty dippers hop and dart from stone-to-stone
like day-trippers gingerly chancing a quick icy paddle

She enters and dazzles the-cathedral city-of Kilkenny
then makes a meek meandering way through Maddockstown.
After endlessly tossing and torrenting here and there,
towards tiny Thomas Town she turns and steadily slows.
Then she ribbons and rushes to enter New Ross
with rippling glee, aching to be engulfed by the sea –
and joyfully joins her beautiful sister Barrow.

They turn and twine together, undivided Siamese twins,
with doubled size and strength their goal determined to win;
they spurt and speed headlong for Waterford's watery scene
rushing like rash sea-maidens to Neptune's waiting harem.

Continued

On the last lap of their jointly joyous race –
with their other long-lost sibling they come face to face;
their snaking sister Suir comes swelling from the West.
Born like Nore in the bosom of the Clonakenny hills
SHE made a meandering path by Thurles and the Golden way,
through Caher town and New Castle she drove and endured,
continuously lured by the scent of the salty sea ahead.
Having long borne their separate lonesome ways
they rush to clasp each other in welcome warm
and forget the long, lonely life of separation.
In sight of Ballyhack three sisters re-unite, on track
to mix and merge with grace into their eternal womb.

CRUX

(St. Fiacre's Church, Loughboy, Kilkenny. Crucifix designed by Oisin Kelly (1915-1981); designer of many national monuments including "Children of Lir" in the Remembrance Gardens in Dublin. In 1964 he was Artist-in-Residence in Kilkenny Design Centre.)

Looking up –
a puzzle there;
no thorny crown
or beads of blood.
Strong features, fatherly face
gazing down,
alert, direct,
no pain-filled frown.

No bony frame,
no pierced palms,
cruel nails,
or injured feet
but sturdy limbs –
solid, secure,
standing firm.

What tale does
sculptor mean to tell?
No visible wounds;
are they cloaked
or overlaid
by overlord sublime
while powerful hands
pour out a silent blessing.

ST. FIACRE 30/3/11

(born end 6th C; died 18 Aug 670; Feast Day 30th Sept.)

Cowled figure, deep in contemplation,
weary with former wanderings to far-off France
to escape Kilkenny's throng and bustle.
The Cadfael of his time, skilled with herbs,
gifted with healing hands – but longing
for a place of quiet solitude – finally found in Breuil.
Built his cell and garden there,
short-lived peace, his spirit moved to
build a house of prayer, then a hospice
for the travel-worn pilgrims of his day –
now known as the village of Saint-Fiacre.

Breuil – At Meaux in the Province of Brie, relics still there.

Village of St. Fiacre – in Seine-et-Marne.

Returned, and settled among the curvy paths
and plant-filled beds of this quiet comer;
surely no Battle King at heart, more likely raven;
content to settle in this peaceful haven
[his spirit uplifted by news of a Green Mayor
spreading the cult of home-grown fruit & veg!]
Fiacre oversees and blesses the busy fingers
of those who strive to create
a little Eden beside his Church,
as he meditates to the soothing murmur
of the ever-trickling curtain of water.

Malcolm Noonan: French cabs called fiacres since mid-17th Century when established near Hotel St. Fiacre in Paris.

Busy taxis cruise by, oblivious of his watchful eye,
unaware of his silent protection.
Women step confidently along the garden paths,
no inkling of his ban against their presence
in his French hermitage and chapel;
p'raps age has lessened his fear of their proximity.

Welcome home, gentle saint, work-worn hands
at rest at last, though spade still at the ready;
no lonely vigil here – a stream of people come and go,
delighted with their thriving Parish Centre.

HOPE

(Famine Exhibition, Kilkenny 2012)

Renovated work house walls watch;
gathered throng admires the art.
Pale wraiths linger longingly
within the shadowy windows.
Students scan their spread-out array,
models of scattered belongings,
battered boxes, tattered trunks –
echoes of families fleeing
from the dreaded, drooping
figure of skeletal Famine.

Scant belongings in the containers
but each holding a portion of hope,
a flicker of life amongst
the dark embers of despair.
On a prominent column
a bright model catches the eye –
a Garden of Remembrance
bursting with life,
bud and leaf of hope.

The shadowy shades watch silently
they all have their memories
families overwhelmed by fierce famine,
relentless wandering ended in an unmarked grave
beneath this crowded amphitheatre.

Perhaps they will be given the chance
to gather around the consolation of their living memorial,
beacon of hope for the future.

PURPLE BEECH

(1750-2002; Castle Gardens, Kilkenny)

Small object nesting on its posh red cushion;
I stroke its smooth honey-coloured surface;
hard to believe it emerged from an ancient tree –
an immigrant planted while George III ruled;
"Methuselah" whose 3 generations spanned three-fifty years,
before its weakened state dictated its demise
this fragment was transformed by Liam's skilful touch.   *Liam Kirwan.*
I turn it over, faintly warm and scan its pale markings,
delicate traces of its ancestral tree rings;
maybe a gentle rubbing will provide a useful
Genii and give imaginations wings
to whiz me back through Time.
Now – to work; this dainty pen has a useful,
modern heart and I must start back to put it
to good use and appreciate its magic transformation.

POSTBOXES – KILKENNY

10/6/2011

Almost unseen tho' accustomed sight,
squatly standing in familiar green,
no UK military red for these professional lads,
shiny great-coat braving rain and wind,
shackled to a solitary spot,
no sentry-box to shelter from the storms
and vagaries of Irish weather.
Some less free but quite content,
wall-prisoned in a stony monkish cell.

A dispersed platoon spanning generations
still display anachronistic badges of office
proclaiming allegiance to long-departed monarchs
unloved by local population.
Folk-memory images of dark suppression
still linger in the shadows.
But who among the daily procession
bearing their precious missives
stop to read these telling signs?

Each post-box mouths a wide welcome,
often listens to whispered stories clasped
in his dark but comforting cave –
festive greetings, fond farewells,
S W A L K or "St. Anthony guide".
Each swallows sorrows and sad lines
and, all too often, envelopes framed in black;
then, all regurgitated, sorted, and cycled
towards their final destinations.

Continued

The gallant Victorian trio
carry echoes of Boer's distant battles
and cruel Crimean events – still
they sit demure as Victoria herself;
but proud chests carry her delicate monogram,
letters curved in a bird-like design
reminiscent of Kells' meandered twinings.
Victorian veteran guarding the Old Court House
suffered modern wounds and damaged hinges –
tinges of anti-authority yobs, or just
the empty-headed vandalism of bored minds.

Enshrined outside Switzir's iron gates –
which still guard the terraced haven
designed for poor women of good repute –
an Edwardian brother, beacon of Peace,
is still in place; he enjoyed the decade of war-free
times until the dreadful European carnage came.

A whole family of Georges display
a no-nonsense label in sturdy block letters.
Many of these duty officers heard
the Easter sounds of bomb and blast,
confused revolt which could not last,
followed by the Kilmainham shots –
sad demise of many patriot names.

Some were deafened by the close and raw
reverberations of deadly fraternal conflict –
ironically mis-named as civil;
still stood solid, remaining through times
when grand mansions burnt and fell,
crumbled like the broken promises of freedom.

Continued

Others felt the tremors of the "war to end all wars"
but suffered again within a score of years
the drumming beat of heavy boots
resounding across the Irish sea.
Not for these veterans the mad-marching
grim goose-stepping or hateful "Heil" salute.

LOUGHBOY'S inexperienced youngster,
innocent of such grim memories,
stands gauche on spindly legs.
Harsh modern lines lack rounded grace
but still youth's carefree demeanour
offers us an eager, friendly face.

This multitude of helpers serve us still
but more and more users desert this slow-mail way;
with lightning keystrokes, moving mouse or pad,
words go winging at the speed of light
by wireless waves, stout cable or satellite.
THESE old stalwarts have more than stood the
passage of time – ah! But for how much longer?

POST BOXES – Postscript

May 2019

One sad day – imagine our consternation –
Loughboy's lad's disappeared from his station;
empty space, no warning, no goodbyes,
no youthful face to greet us – maybe this weak-legged
lad had been dismissed, unfit for duty.

We move away and walk, deep in thought still,
to get our pensions, order currency, pay our bills.
And there, outside our local Postal Office,
appears a knowing, modern lad, slim & strong,
guarding the modern door of this thriving P.O.

Already accustomed to the clues of change, he remains
unmoved by a mother with one-handed grip on pushchair,
eyes glued to hand-held phone, talking to her heart's content,
while tiny child's eyes are fully fixed on a miniature screen.
Our lad keeps a watchful eye on constant flow of passers-by –
underage teens chancing their luck to enter betting shop,
laden school kids heaving heavy bags of books
to enter the Library – haven of information & peace.

THE NEW ROAD

Garry duff, Paulstown (2010)

Anxiously scan the window view –
Blackstair's graceful flowing form,
sunken deep in dark despair behind the thrusting harshness
of this powerful intruder whose bare-faced nakedness
is now softly skirted with mellow wooden fence,
sloped sides clothed in green but stony heart cannot be disguised.
Some relief that Leinster's peak can still peer this way,
allow just a glimpse of her changeable moods.
But when trucks and lorries begin to lunge along this route
a noisy silent-movies flickering scene is all that will remain.

F – KHALIL GIBRAN

(Khalil Gibran – writer, poet, artist/
illustrator, philosopher,
b. in Bsharri, Lebanon
6/1/1883; d. 10/4/1931)

THOUGHTS

All of his life he was deeply moved
by Nature's golden treasure,
sometimes it overwhelmed him so,
almost too rich for human measure.

If just ONE star, ONE tree, ONE flower
was left on earth below –
then would we be aware, he said,
God's generous giving really know.

A friendship makes a poem, he said,
a song that never dies,
a new invisible force it creates
which then throughout the Universe sighs.

He shared with his friends the simple joys
life holds for every one
and showed only them his impish self
when all their daily work was done.

Sometimes, he said, they spoilt him so,
wanting to give him too much –
he followed their feasting by fasting alone
then only bread and soup would touch.

His keen advice to each of us
in everything we do
is "keep it simple", be strong, sincere
and most of all be true.

He cared about the plight of mankind
to such a draining extent
that in the end, whilst still quite young,
the whole of his giving was spent.

Continued

'Twas like a light that burned so bright
to show the traveller his way,
it could not last for very long –
a heavy price he had to pay.

But still his lucid thoughts live on
to help mankind and show
the struggling souls who travel still
the testing path on earth below.

So words like his will pass on down
forever through the ages;
his pearls of wisdom still shine out
from the little black book's pages.

GIBRAN'S REQUEST

Gibran's tender thoughts emerged
in the early poems he wrote;
some lines from "Jesus Knocks at the Gates"
are heart-warming here to quote.

He speaks as Jesus asking his Father
to open wide the gates
to welcome in the sorry souls
with all their frail and piteous traits.

"I bring with me the crucified thief
who died with me this day;
I also bring a killer to you
who hunted meat, but man did slay."

Another was a drunkard sad
who thirsted for another world;
he gazed deep down into his glass
as down and down the liquid swirled.

Another was a woman fair
who gave herself to "love".
Men wished to punish her with death,
not so the Son of God above.

A fourth unfortunate was a fool
who gambled all his money;
his dreams were broken into shreds,
he found no land of milk and honey.

All these souls condemned by men
to the gates of heaven he brought.
He loved them all in spite of sin
and mercy from his Father sought.

Continued

The killer was an unwise man
"with twilight on his face",
the woman lived the sort of life
which only brought dis-grace.

The drunkard was a lonely man
who suffered a desolate blindness
but showed the depth of his human heart
by crying when anyone offered him kindness.

He ends the poem with rejoicing great
when the gates are opened wide
"There are no sinners left on earth"
now that these souls are safely inside".

GIBRAN'S LEBANON

When Gibran spoke of his country so fair
his voice would sometimes choke;
he longed to see it strong and free
from every foreign oppressor's yoke.

Whilst still of very tender years,
of freedom he wrote, and urged
that his burdened fellow-countrymen
from all injustice should be purged.

From the leaders and the Maronite Church
a swift response it came
to label him a troublesome one –
a rebel guilty of treason and blame.

By then he was valued in other lands
where his gifts were becoming known;
his sculpture, drawings and paintings rare
the seeds of interest and truth had sown.

His poems too began to take shape
and his mother's views he sought;
her gentle reply was oft of the kind
which perseverance and patience taught.

"Later", she said, "just place it aside;
for haste there is no need,"
and so, to "whip and prune" over time
became his habit and his creed.

The early lines of "The Prophet" he wrote
while still of tender years;
it talks of truth, religion and work,
of beauty, children, marriage, fears.

Continued

Its pages are filled with thoughts profound
and truth as old as the hills
which homes like an arrow direct to the heart
and then one's very being fills.

To discover this book is a source of delight
which never fails to inspire;
it helps one to look afresh at life
and fan faith's embers into new fire.

G – NATURE

SPRING

The first spurt of joy rises in surprise as
tiny clumps of snow-drops come magically into view;
cold, clammy grasp of winter begins to release,
all around creation awakes and begins to renew.

Dainty almond blossoms from nowhere appear,
and a spiky shrub seemingly not worth a glance,
bare in its leafless state, suddenly sprouts forsythia –
miraculous mass of yellow bloom our spirits to elate.

POPLARS

(St. Canice's Hospital, Kilkenny)

Joy in a place of peace,
wind-breaks for the stony buildings
huddled all around.
Even here poplars parade
in military style –
echo of France's sentinelled roads;
continental cousins once deafened by the tumult
of a thousand marching men;
lopped and mis-used
for Napoleonic hordes,
re-cycled to carry death's load
of heavy booming cannon.
Here – they safely stretch,
miniscule leaves fluttering
in the slightest breeze;
slender uprights, straight & tall;
like the suffering inmates
returned from that hellish war,
they're able to enjoy a place of peace.

THE DAMSEL FLY

[Dedicated to my sister Veronica RIP; remembering our visit to BUNANAUGH (Bottom of the Ford) Streamstown, Co. Westmeath – 1983/4]

We found fields of luscious pasture,
we found flowers without number
scattered like the stars in heaven,
twinkling wide-eyed without slumber.

We saw armies of straight nettles
standing sentinel around us,
banks of brier in tangled islands
midst the mass of green-leafed lilies.

We felt clusters of spiked thistles
as we tip-toed our way thro' them,
from the countless cups of butter
we were warmed by yellow sun-glow.

We felt joy surge through our spirits
as a rich and rolling carpet
dotted o'er with sun-drenched daisies
turned their radiant faces t'wards us.

We smelt scent of many flowers
midst the new-washed grass aroma
and the hedgerows subtle fragrance
mixed with bon-fires smoky odour.

Smoky sun-baked cattle pancakes
spread their essence ever downward
cycling back life-giving contents
to Nature's hidden creatures,

leaching past the rocks and rubble
in and out the ant and mole hills
through the hordes of busy insects
down among the rich root endings.

Continued

We heard gentle lowing cattle
and the sound of varied bird-song
long or short notes, sharp, or winding
like a woven web of sound-threads.

We heard distant drone of tractors
and the crash of heavy planking
echo in the distant spaces
from a world so far away.

In the stillness came a faint sound –
hum of dainty fairy damsel
flitting nimbly midst the flowers
darting down among the daisies.

We caught glimpses of wings pearly,
blue and shimmering in the sunshine,
shades of sky, and sea, and turquoise,
flitting, floating, vivid rainbow.

We heard bubbling, babbling water
as the sparkling stream flowed by us
gushing, gurgling in the bright light
rushing rashly t'wards the Shannon.

Wandering water, oft meandering
'tween the mossy banks of green,
home for fishes of quick silver
lightning flashes barely seen,

in among the smoothed pebbles
up and down o'er sun-bleached stones
washed by centuries of water
to the whiteness of dried bones.

Thrusting thro' the reeds and rushes
tumbling down the tiny torrents
speeding with the surging water
constant searching ever sea-ward.

THE FALL

A chilly breeze begins to blow,
restless rustling amidst the trees,
an increased fall of dying leaves,
cast-off stitches slipped from needles.

Temperature drops, wind rises
whines and whistles, cuts with cold,
rain drops splatter, leaves scatter,
colonies abruptly cast adrift.

Whirling eddies out of control,
coracles on a choppy sea
shaken and shuffled like paper scraps
in colourful kaleidoscopes of old.

They quiver and shiver, get shifted along
relentlessly roving, and re-arranged
like rootless vagrants who nowhere belong
from their beginnings completely estranged,

winding and weaving a wandering way
travelling blindly without stable form
whipping and skipping like children at play
endlessly tossed on life-journey's storm.

After churning and turning, finally resting
or kids kicking thoughtlessly through
with lively, undisguised delight
as only children easily do.

Continued

Some are gathered like golden grain
racked and raked, bagged and baked,
(smells of smoky bonfires stray).
Others spread, underfoot crunch,
wither and weather, earthworms munch,
mutely make their contribution
to re-nourish the earth without a say.

AUTUMN IMAGES

HORSE CHESTNUT

Horse chestnut hands hang overhead
a jaundiced tinge comes into view
and day by day begins to spread
until they're enveloped in golden hue.
Prickly-skinned spheres burst asunder
releasing highly polished surprises –
reddish-brown balls for school-boy battles,
pierced and strung, raised and swung
in determined hands for hard-won prizes.

PLANE TREE

The towering plane tree, head held high,
stretches its leaf-laden arms like sails;
its myriad leaves softly edged
with yellow, like gold-tipped finger nails.
Red patches appear, and creep along –
they seep and darken into rusty rashes,
russet splashes contrast with the gold
to transform later into leaf-mould.

A single leaf drifts silently down
and lies alone in solitary splendour,
its perfect pattern mounted clear
against the grass's greeny gown.
Soon other playmates break their bonds
and zig-zag down to join their fellow,
sailing like miniature magic carpets
of rusty red or ochre yellow.

SUMACH

The Sumach stands in deep-green livery
elfin-brushed with reddish touches
which over-night appear to spread
like modest maiden's crimson blushes;
brilliant bursts of orangey red
echo the Bible's burning bush,
fiery coals, goldfish shoals
fairy lights illumining night.

BEECH

The rustling beech shows yellow streaks
and copper throngs which gleam and glow,
blazon into burnished bronze,
flutter and float to the earth below
and weave a multi-coloured rug
snug and warm, rich and mellow.

SYCAMORE

The sycamore's webbed fingers bright,
glowing embers in a dying fire
as if festooned with fire-flies' light
(without awaiting the dark of night).
From among the flaming red-rust clusters
some to the ground sink slowly swooning,
dis-connected, shed for ever,
silent descent, cold-air ballooning
to gather below in melancholy musters.

BIRDS

KINGFISHER

(inspired by "Study of a Kingfisher", a painting by John Ruskin (1819-1900)

Short and small of stature as you are
breath-taking beauty, iridescent jewel,
flashing colours far outstripping rainbow hues,
keen of eye and still as silent shadow
until the prey appears, a glint of silver
in the surging stream below.
Then arrow-like you shoot
and catch the unsuspecting minnow;
arising in a rush of thrilling triumph,
fast-beating wings spread myriad
drops of water, memory's image
blowing miniature magic bubbles.
Have you hidden your precious treasures
in a vole-like hole in nearby river bank?
Our spirits soar and harbour halcyon hopes
that life and weather speak of tranquil days.

THE SWIFTS

(dedicated to Mairead who loves the house martins who I always mistook for swifts!!)

Triangular-pointed wings of *swifts* swooping fast
evoke misty memories of summers longtime past.
Like hordes of joyous spirits they fly wild and free,
fleet figures fleeing and darting there and here.

They play an unplanned game of swooping tag,
dip and dive in and out the telephone wires,
under eaves, and through the trees, they take the air
through summer's busy insect hum, without a care.

Continued

They choose mates, build in every conceivable place –
roofs, barns and sheds, in a hole, on a slender ledge;
in and out they dip and dart at an unbelievable pace,
nest and nurture their fledglings and see them well fed
then gradually build up strength for the arduous journey ahead.

As time passes swiftly by and summer sun is spent,
they gather in gossiping groups on fence, wire and roof,
natter a newsy exchange and twitter without reproof;
chirp and chit-chatter before their gruelling flight.

Of a sudden, as if of one mind, they depart one night;
rise surely and swiftly on fast-fluttering wings, soar up to the sky
towards the horizon, wings waving an annual goodbye;
they head south, fast, for the white chalky cliffs of Dover;
our spirits suffer a tinge of sadness – summer is over.

THE SPARROW

Cheeky London sparrow – tame and bright of eye,
quietly propelled by stubby neatly-flapping wings,
bravely buzzing in among the bigger birds,
perfectly prepared with them for food to vie.
Hopping here and there to capture every crumb,
cheerful chirpy creature, seems without a care;
in winter frosty chill or sunny summer hum
zealously zooming in on every ledge and sill.
Dull drab-coated in the people-polluted air
though sun shows flashes of subtle shade and hue,
wings subtly barred with deep brown and beige
in Spring black bib he dons, determined to ensure
his lively little mate will notice and pursue –
plucky little flier, his chances he can gauge.

Continued

Stealthily stepping, sneakily snaffling every speck,
braving the greedy starlings ill-tempered peck,
undeterred by winter's cupboard cold and bare
not prepared for frost's creeping cruel chill
his tiny offspring to overcome and quietly kill.

THE BLACKBIRD

Glossy, dark-black coat, beak of yellow
bright-eyed and alert, this fleet-footed fellow
startled or disturbed by creature large or small
swiftly sounds a sudden sharp warning call.
When undisturbed, its little heart no longer pounds –
trilling, piercing blackbird song carries clear,
one can hear it loud above the traffic sounds,
singing out his heart in praise of God's creation;
brown partner gathering twigs and insects fat
for their tiny nestlings,
hears his message of joyous elation.

THE OVIDS

(dedicated to Tessa)

CROWS

The clumsy-gaited often-hated crow
often a solitary, slow-moving figure,
a waddling old man with heavy paunch,
hoarse-voiced, harsh-sounding loner,
awesome and lonesome a figure as ancient Jonah,
thought to bring tidings full of woe –
derided and disliked, striking fear
in beating hearts of humans living near.

Continued

Secret stories of scary magic powers,
connection with sooth-sayer or seer.
How this subtle seed was widely sown
we do not know but root and thrive it did –
misty memories from which the spirit cowers,
mysterious tales spread and oft related.

Ebony coat with reflections purple and green
this strong and striking bird wasn't fated
to be shunned, hated and reviled;
like all creatures, consciously created,
that a useful role it has is clear –
seeking dead an'decayed from far and near.

Like the rook it can be very helpful –
they steadfastly search out and destroy
"leather jackets" which ruin the roots of grain,
persistent pests that the farmer fights in vain –
craneflies, known to us as Daddy Longlegs.

The hooded crows have very similar habits
though their mantle and underparts are grey;
their vocal sounds less harsh people say
and more varied, may even pass for song
but most humans wouldn't listen very long!

ROOKS

Rooks are crows' raucous-voiced relations;
black garb with violet and blue gloss.
They gather together in noisy garrulous groups
like travellers in over-crowded stations.

Their bill noticeably longer and more pointed,
conspicuous bare white skin around its base
make it easier to recognise their face
an' distinguish them from their similar cousins.

Continued

75

Gregarious spirits, in colonies they build
their busy rookery nurseries in tall trees;
they love to caw in chorus without cease,
unlikely to overawe us – or to please.

RAVENS

Larger cousins, the highly renowned ravens,
said to hold deep secrets fast,
stood a centuries-long sentinel duty
at the tall majestic White Tower of London
famous and feared place of embattled beauty.
Their first vigil, Celtic mythology said,
was to guard Bran's decapitated Head –
like the Oracle at Delhi, the nation it guided,
times of crisis, inspired wisdom provided;
though the eyes finally closed for ever
the Ravens still stand watch on the Tower;
'tis said by some they are due to leave it never.

*Bran – story told
in "Mabinogion"
cycle of Welsh
legend.*

MAGPIES

When striking plumage black and white is spied,
the pied member of the ovid family is here,
stream-lined shape, graceful wedge-tipped tail –
in full flowing flight, an eye-catching sight,
brief glimpses of fast, flashing white.
Well-known is the magpie's link with prediction –
a pair seen together, augurs well –
fine weather is sure to follow soon.
Their lively spirits are not easy to quell
they love glistening, glittering objects or gems –
avid collectors, renowned jewel thieves;
often found in their nest among the leaves
glass or diamond ring, or silver spoon.

THE COUNTRYSIDE

(Summer 1990)

An endless quilt of patchwork mainly gold and green
securely sewn, stitched into place with dark-hued hedges
dividing deftly multi-angled shapes and squares
and neatly knitting the hazy horizon's outer edges.

An undulating counterpane of cosy hills
with dinky dwellings nestling in the bosomy folds
dotted with grazing sheep and cattle, and stone-slabbed mills
under a grey shrouded canopy of rainy drape.

Rich bark-brown fields in stitched segments set;
previously ploughed, disc-harrowed to loosen lumpy clods,
left bare, to weather, rain-soak and then fine harrow the sods;
now lying in wait for drilling, open-mouthed ready for seed.

Golden cornfields with smooth sculpted tracks like rails,
parallel curves etched in endless snaking trails;
comfy curved pillows of brilliant oil-seed rape;
fields filled with giant flaxen cotton-reel bales.

WEEPING WILLOWS

(Wandsworth Common, Battersea; July 1998)

A corner of Wandsworth Common, a triangular stretch of green,
a magnificent weeping willow, most massive ever seen,
in rapt attention spreads soft protective arms
over the swings and shrubs comprising the sunlit scene.
Its smaller sisters, too, each have their task to do –
swaying limbs sweep over the ground below them.
They crouch down closer to the dusty earth below;
one watches closely children on the pendulum swings,
the little rocking duck, the circling round-about;

their hanging hands hold them safe like Guardian wings
whilst they swing secure above the safe, soft-surfaced floor.
From the lofty top of St. Marks' unseen spiky steeple
a lone figure watches over the unaware people
who all dwell under the voiceless cockerel's gaze.
The children play while adults gain a moment's laze.
The second sister's slender fingers fondly caress
the chattering children entirely engrossed in endless play,
softly smoothing all their everyday cares away;
a happy haven, a peaceful corner carers bless.

Her swirling masses of golden-green tresses stroke the ground,
sheltering small charges avidly playing seek and hide
under the welcome umbrella of low, hanging locks
strealing down like luxuriant hair waiting to be tied.
In Spring a magical multitude of shoots appear in the grounds,
a floor-covering carpet creeping across the grassy mounds.
Suddenly they sprout into thousands of sun-coloured heads –
nodding and tossing with glee beside the still-asleep beds.
They tread and spread across the undulating hills –
merry skipping masses of dancing daffodils.

H – MEMORIES

THE HARVEST

(dedicated to Liam and Ruairi who loved watching the harvester when they were small)

Harvest monster chugs across the cloth of gold,
slashing swathes of stalks into his gaping mouth,
swallows, and swills them into his churning stomach bold,
swirling, rolly-polly-ing them into huge bales;
then speedily spurts them out on to the spiky ground,
gigantic golden reels of grain regurgitated there
to settle and sun-bathe dry in the elusive summer air,
whilst strips of straw and seeds are scattered all around.
When weariness finally finds the mighty fearsome beast
and his heavy metal body comes to a silent stop –
a multitude of birds descend for this free feast,
raucous rooks and crows by the hundred peck and hop.

SUMMER PLAY

(10/99: Dedicated to Liam & Ruairi who loved to play among the bales of hay when they were small)

Below the long, long length of hedge
an uncut field of golden hay;
a jungle world for kids to play.
Hidden monsters well-imagined,
childish dramas fondly fashioned.

In front of the long, long length of hedge
grass grew high and thick
until the tractor chugged along,
chopped and cut the dried golden hay
then rolled it into giant bales.

Beyond the long, long length of hedge,
when the combine's work was done,
for a few dazzling days
golden bales lay bathing in the sun –
a source of play for two small boys.
Hoisted high to ride the reel,
the scratchy feel fully favoured
close contact with the earth's yield;
in the curving field yellow leftovers –
a new experience keenly savoured.

Tiny tiger imitators,
growling gruffly in mock ferocity,
camouflaged in the undergrowth,
then hurtling forth with high velocity
to scare the pants off all nearby.

WHISPERS

(Shurock, Castletown Geo.)

A solitary cottage comes suddenly into view
slumbering at the edge of the curving country road;
sad smokeless chimneys, vacant-eyed shell
choked and over-come with dogged creeping weeds
Sombre slates long replaced the golden thatch
atop three tiny rooms innocent of all mod-cons;
forlorn ancient range rusted and dusty with age
whispers the passage of time, impressions of long ago.
Fingers tenderly trace a track through the dust of the
rough hewn dresser decked with earthen dishes,
stacked with a fascinating fund of pots, pictures,
mugs and jugs, medals and black rosary beads.
Now, drawers littered with flittered paper scraps,
once prized possessions of those who lived within,
sad remains of newspaper cuttings, faded letters.
Sharp-toothed rodents raided the undisturbed depths
like Time himself devouring all and wreaking devastation.
Sad-eyed, crumpled Sacred Heart still gazes down,
shadowy expressions flitting over his pale face
in faint and flickering light of the sole candle below,
arms spread ready for a warm embrace,
uncovering the fiery glow of his unwavering love.
We stand and stare and sigh and think of times long past,
accepting that nothing solid lasts – save Truth and Love.
We turn around and take the track which leads us back
– to the future.

DREAMS

Frail fragments of reality,
scattered wide to the winds,
gathered and gleaned in doleful dreams,
pieced together like a Picasso –
lop-sided faces, strange places,
mixed together in impossible ways.

People we meet, know the name
but here the face is not the same;
hearing voices we cannot hear,
seeing people we cannot see –
gone from us for evermore.

Days glimpsed through a haze,
things of deep, darkest night
struggling through a confusing maze;
some events creepy and scary
or vague warnings to make us wary.

Hidden springs surging up
from a deep source within;
dreams drawing up a cup
from a well deeply hidden;
forgotten hurts slyly emerging,
sidling up to us unbidden.

Invisible seeds begin to sprout,
determined to find their way out;
if we can but look direct
and dare our delicate soul to bare,
accept the unacceptable truth, then
serenity they cannot wreck.

SCATTER BRAIN

Children romp, forget the time,
lose their coats, forget their notes,
leave their precious books behind.
"Scatter-brain!", the parents say.
Now, sudden gaps in everyday talk,
words disappear, hide from view,
even names well-known to you,
fumbling around, can't be found.
We know well they're really there,
index cards filed away
in memory's depths from the light of day.

Words lurk just out-of-sight;
you feel such a birk, word is near;
"it's on the tip of the tongue" we say;
heart beats, thoughts compete.
Give up, let go! Then what-do'ya know –
out of the blue, when back is turned,
teasing word pops into view.
One of our battles finally won
but maybe the war has hardly begun.
"Scatter brain," the children say.

IMPRESSIONS

the way that rays slant through the trees
the way some people put us at ease
the emotions stirred by an image fine
the sudden standing still of time
the echo of a distant song
the feeling that we really belong
the little things that please us so
the friends we feel we really know

the face that fleetingly shows a change
the angry tone of a voice we know
the hurt of a friend's untimely blow
the shiver that shakes us when we fear
the feeling that something bad is near
the awful awaiting for the 'phone
the answer that chills us to the bone
the news that fills our hearts with dread

the knowledge something bad's been said
the friendship broken by a wedge
the unspoken words, the broken pledge
the instinct that we caused offence
the unease we feel about pretence
the dilemma that a friendship's ended
the puzzle that can't be comprehended
the sense that someone is silently sorry

the regret that we have caused a worry
the instinct that a storm is brewing
the feeling that Faith needs renewing
the sense that we're always in need of prayer
the warm feeling of someone near to care
the relief that He is always there
that hidden help is always near so
the sense of evil we need not fear.

AIR RAIDS

An early memory – sheets of paper black –
mourning signs before the patient's dead –
pinned with care to cover every window,
shut in every light, allow no slack,
essential to seal the slightest crack.

Our first retreat – Anderson shelter small –
five humans and a friendly, smelly dog –
conditions cramped in a corrugated cave,
below ground, a cold metal wall,
two wooden planks to sit upon.

Some nights spent sitting on cellar stairs
lips low-tone talking, ears stretching
intent to catch sky-sounds distant above.
Endless scary banshee stories –
unerring attempts to bind our attention.

Faint sound of planes; ours or theirs the question
that hangs unspoken in the tensioned air.
Faces uplifted mime a voiceless prayer,
silence broken by faint diesel drone –
feared, familiar throbbing rhythm nears
and fans the flame of hidden human fears,
listening for whistling whine of bombs descending.

One unforgettable night we heard them all too clearly –
ground shook and rumbled like a 'quake;
our windows broke, some people paid more dearly.
In the morning light, an unbelievable sight –
nearby corner site completely crumbled –
the tall Eye Hospital dis-appeared that night
and later re-emerged as our Co-op.

Continued

The high-pitched unrelenting siren sounds,
someone out of their cosy bed bounds
to wake the weary log-like figures around;
shaken from sleep, thoughts dis-connected,
clothes carelessly thrown on, still half-asleep
dragging dozey feet along the darkened street.

Reluctant to enter the reinforced shelter –
under-shop, underground claustrophobic base;
tunnels wall-to-wall with triple-tier bunks,
bodies layered like sardines crammed;
sleep-seeking unwanted unwounded moans,
cramped bones, low muted tones,
some sleep-talking or deep dream walking.
Oh! for an undisturbed peace-filled night.

Another time, in weather bright and fine,
we heard their spine-chilling whistle and whine
- a devastating crop of bombs fell down nearby
and then a jarring, stomach-churning thud.
At last the All Clear siren sounded out,
back to bed we thankfully crawled
not knowing what dawn would reveal.

Next day a jumbled tangle, a rubbled mess;
a family of friends in dismal dis-array –
mother blasted dead, guarding the cot,
one twin cold, the other sitting unscathed – just
sat quiet in his cot, never cried –
a single scratch upon his chubby face;
the father fatally injured, later died.

We loved the twins, and often played with them.
How could this be, we couldn't comprehend;
we didn't know on life one can't depend –
the end may be nearby, hidden from view.
The ghastly games the politicians play,
what rules they use, we really couldn't say.

Continued

Unaware we were of other suffering people –
Hull, Berlin, Coventry and Dresden.
We only knew that this should never happen –
suffering, paralysed state, check-mate;
we longed to re-create a new world;
the unrealistic, prophesied six-months
for all became an ever-lasting wait.

But memories of those times are not all bleak
mostly life ran on in its usual way –
tears, and laughter, work and even play.
VE Day, street parties, jam and jelly,
playing tag and carefree hide-and-seek;
food was short but still enough to eat.

Nowadays we need to remember all those things
and say a prayer of thanks for every moment,
for every little joy that comes our way,
for children's trustful eyes turned towards us,
for bursting buds and shady tree overhead,
for birds' joyful song and flashing wings
and a good night's sleep in our own welcome bed.

MOVING HOUSE

Only bricks and mortar lifeless and dry,
no visible bond to tie us to this place,
just memories flutter in and out our minds,
shades from dimming past, flitting fast,
flashing across our inward cine-screen,
tease us with thoughts of long ago,
forcefully pull us back to scattered scenes
we thought forgotten, souls begotten,
those unborn who slipped away unseen,
borne on wings of welcoming cherub throngs
whose soothing song was silent to our ears.
Here our bonny, sturdy babes grew strong
belonging to this world of temporary stay.

We happily choose to go, don't feel uprooted,
excitement muted by the presences pale
who steadfastly refuse to disappear,
memories unlocked by saddening farewells.
We never recognised them in the melée
of normal everyday life and crowded living,
not giving a thought to far-off trials and times
or chimes of life's incessant ceaseless clock.
But soothed by the familiar things surrounding us
we pack with care, though still aware
of slumbering images who tug at memory.
We gently fold and lay them away again
into the recesses of our inner being.
Looking forward is the way to go,
we know how blessed the years have been to us
and so we trust the hidden route ahead.

TREE OF LIGHT

(Veronica's painting; Diprose Lodge, Garrett Lane, London – 1999)

We ambled around that precious space –
a private place
allowing rare moments of togetherness,
to stroll in sombre silence
or relax in an exchange of scarce words.
Two sisters sharing,
still striving to overcome the past effects
on families split by illness and war,
and to strengthen a fragile relationship.

But at this time and in this place
it was easier to understand
the ruffled ripples of the previous years,
the silent shedding of our hidden tears.
We knew that Time was running out
but could not know how soon
his unpredictable scythe would strike.

And now I often gaze
at what we thought an ordinary tree.
Veron's rare talent and deft hand
made a new creation –
breath-taking beacon of ethereal,
effervescent glow
emerging out of a pool of yellow light.
The glowing arms stretch out
their luminous fingers
to bestow a silent blessing
on the little terraced houses
where a tiny chapel gem nestles in their midst.

ALMSHOUSES

(1848 Diprose Lodge, Tooting; 1998)

An oasis of tranquillity created by Clement Danes,
in the year of '48 alone it grew;
now it nestles in between grey granite blocks
and encircling spires of lonely local churches
(still proudly parading high-perched weather vanes)
long since empty – or peopled by the few.

A group of cosy houses, strongly strung together
(each containing tiny, winding sets of stairs)
with diamond-patterned walls of brick and staggered stone,
overseen by cowled chimneys thrusting t'wards the stars,
stretching to the heavens high above the zone.

Door-steps cheerily painted carmine Cardinal red,
wide windows with a view many a neighbour envies,
boot-scrapers in the wall, to clean the tread
of high-buttoned boots before the time of wellies.

Little pillared porches give respite from rain,
like cloistered lay-bys tho' they give scant shelter
(the wind whines and whistles through their iron bars)
carefully locked 'gainst stranger or intruder
as well as unruly children running helter-skelter.

NAMES

Names scratched in the bark of a tree,
hearts entwined as if forever.
Words written in the sand
washed away by the incoming sea,
friendship which was only skin-deep
which we thought would fail us never.

Names etched in solid stone,
some events upon us imprinted,
solid and lasting as coins minted;
others fleeting, unrepeated,
footsteps furrowed in the sand,
blown away by the winds' command.

Cruel names can be sculpted deep;
if allowed, our soul they singe
and leave a tinge of bitterness.
Like thorns, sarcastic comments tear,
scour and score, leaving victims sore
and their psyche scarred with weals
which need love and gentle care.

FRIENDSHIP

(dedicated to Babs & Rita – Easter 2005) "Friendship makes a poem, a song that never dies." Kahlil Gibran)

To know the open ease of being who you are
without the constant caution of one's close encounters
when closest kin seem not to know us well at all.
How can we tell them of our own deep-hidden needs,
the seeds unconsciously sown long lives ago.

We know a loving bond beneath the surface lies
but can be clouded by the cutting word or just
the ordinary cut and thrust of everyday life,
rife in every person's solitary journey Home.

Bending backwards to be seen fair and just
does not always success ensure, no magic cure
comes to soothe the injured soul or softly smooth
the ruffled feathers of the precious ones we love.

'Tis then God's gift to humankind we truly value,
when feelings run amok and the morrow's hard to face
without a smear of balm, or trace of understanding,
we can appreciate that Fate has sent us Friendship.

Varied terraces of trust we yearly build
from easy surface chat to deeply opening up
to dare and share a cup of sorrow or of joy
to nourish our fragile self-belief or soothe our grief.

Refreshed we can return to the challenging situation,
avoid sharing our gift of unrequested advice,
look far beyond the failings our experienced eye can see;
instead respond to the unspoken plea for recognition.

Continued

Maybe then the most our tutored lips should utter
are thoughts to affirm each struggling soul behind their mask,
our task to forget the past, build up upon the best
and leave the rest in our Saviour's sympathetic hands.

ORACLE

(dedicated to my sister Veronica RIP; impressions of her painting "Oracle")

Young-old face of humanity,
wide-eyed innocent full of hope
yet often dragged t'wards dark despair.
Striving for peace, unsettled by war,
pale and shell-shocked features wan,
priest-priestess, trivia-shorn,
sick, heartsore, consumed with longing
for peace and love to govern all.

Solitary sitter, still as night,
wounded wraith with patient faith,
unenigmatic silent Sphinx
gazing across evershifting sand
that blurs the difficult path ahead,
the storms that unexpected rise
and blind the tired travellers' eyes,
landscape swept and shaped by Fate.

A-sexual symbol of heart's desire,
stretching, reaching out of earth's mire.
Life-endowing tearlets fall,
crystal tear-drops, sadly shed,
gather gradually into a stream –
the measure of human misery and pain;
tear-stained visage suffering still
but fearlessly focussed on hope ahead.

LAST JOURNEY

(3/7/99 Dedicated to Veronica RIP)

Entering the room with cautious tread
like reverent walking on hallowed ground.
Friends come and go and sit around,
sounds subdued, low-tone talking.

High-perched bed like a child's cot
with side arms to cradle safely;
inert figure quietly sleeps
while wakeful watch guardians keep.

Gentle kiss on a burning brow,
hiss of oxygen like distant rain,
whir of fan to cool the air,
drip of life to ease any pain.

We gently sponge the peaceful face
and reassure that we are there.
We talk together of other times
and other places we have seen.

The Seaford front, the Pompey shores,
the Rhododendron wood with scores
of multi-coloured blooms in sight
to swell our hearts with sheer delight.

We marvel at the battle fought
so hard and long in these past years,
the awe-inspiring courage shown,
overcoming all setbacks and fears.

We listen to the shallow breathing
and turn to God for what is best;
the pain of loss is sharp within us
but still we pray for final rest.

Continued

Familiar verses come to mind
De Profundis, hear my voice
out of the depths we cry to thee
only He can make the choice.

Low-voiced staff pad in and out,
caring and quiet, comfort-giving,
carefully checking all through the night
unobtrusive, but always about.

Open curtains, night view,
terraced houses, rooftops and trees,
chimneys, shops and moving traffic,
street lamps shining through.

Faint light over-head
as life-force flickers and gradually dims,
breathing slows and starts to ease,
no need now for fear or dread.

Just across the hospital wall
a world apart and unaware,
sleeping souls without a thought –
oblivious of the Final Call.

As shadows diminish and dawn peeps,
pink seeps over the sky;
we sit and wait for death to come
but no grim reaper we await.

Just a silent rustling in the still air,
a loving presence to dispel all care;
angel wings gently swoop
and softly scoop the waiting soul.

The spirit soft ready to go,
to swiftly soar to heaven's gate,
to meet all those who there await;
all our goodbyes are finally said.

Continued

Gudavis, Gudavis, God be with you
to guide you along that passage bright
and see you safely through that door
where your star will be shining evermore.